BEYOND 2000
GENETIC ENGINEERING

Redrawing the Blueprint of Life

BEYOND 2000
GENETIC ENGINEERING

Redrawing the Blueprint of Life

by David Darling

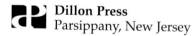
Dillon Press
Parsippany, New Jersey

Acknowledgments

The author wishes to thank Wendy McGoodwin, of the Council for Responsible Genetics and managing editor of GeneWatch, and Dr. Stuart Newman, of the Department of Cell Biology and Anatomy, New York Medical College, for their many expert comments and criticisms during the preparation of this book.

Photo Credits

COVER: © Sinclair Stammers/Science Photo Library/Photo Researchers, Inc.
© Secchi-Lecague/Roussel-Oclaf/CNRI/Science Photo Library/Photo Researchers, Inc.: 5, 11, 23, 34, 42, 52. Monsanto: 7, 8, 46, 50. National Medical Slide Bank: 10, 35, 54. © David Leah/Science Photo Library/Photo Researchers, Inc.: 13. ©DRI/Science Photo Library/Photo Researchers, Inc.: 18. © A. Barrington Brown/Photo Researchers, Inc.: 22. © Hattie Young/Science Photo Library/Photo Researchers, Inc.: 24. © Will & Deni McIntyre/Photo Researchers, Inc.: 30. © Martin Dohrn/IVF UNIT, Cromwell Hospital/Science Photo Library/Photo Researchers, Inc.: 32. ©Philippe Plailly/Science Photo Library/Photo Researchers, Inc.: 33, 43. AFRC/David Darling: 48. © Catherine Pouedras/Science Photo Library/Photo Researchers, Inc.: 55. © Alfred Pasieka/Science Photo Library/Photo Researchers, Inc.: 59. Illustrations by Marie T. Dauenheimer: 12, 15, 17, 19, 21, 27, 38.

Library of Congress Cataloging-in-Publication Data

Darling, David J.
    Genetic engineering: redrawing the blueprint of life/by David Darling.—
1st ed.
      p. cm.—(Beyond 2000)
    Includes bibliographical references and index.
    ISBN 0-87518-614-9   ISBN 0-382-24952-6 pbk
    1. Genetic engineering—Juvenile literature. [1. Genetic engineering.] I. Title. II. Series.
QH442.D37   1995
575.1'0724—dc20

                                              94-28652

Summary: Explores the recent developments in genetic engineering, describing the workings of the cell and DNA, the efforts made in the realm of gene therapy and genetic counseling, and the controversial issues surrounding this emerging area of science.

Published by Dillon Press, an imprint of Silver Burdett Press.
A Simon & Schuster Company
299 Jefferson Road, Parsippany, NJ 07054

First edition

Printed in Mexico

10 9 8 7 6 5 4 3 2 1

CONTENTS

Introduction

Imagine that we could put an end to some of the most crippling diseases and disabilities with which children are born. Imagine, too, that we could create new animals and plants to help solve some of the world's most urgent problems. Cows might be altered to produce life-saving drugs in their milk. Tiny organisms might be made that could convert garbage into fuel. Or new types of plants might be grown that could absorb more carbon dioxide from the air and so help prevent global warming.

Crops that produce their own pesticides as they grow have been among the first practical developments of genetic engineering.

The large boll on the left comes from a cotton plant that was genetically engineered to fend off damaging insect pests. The boll on the right is from an unaltered plant that has been attacked by insects.

Although breakthroughs such as these would once have seemed impossible, they are now close to becoming real. Over the last 40 years, scientists have learned a great deal about the chemical changes taking place inside living things. They have deciphered the code by which animals and plants pass on their characteristics to their offspring. They have even learned how to alter that code to produce life-forms with new characteristics. The means by which they are able to do this is known as **genetic engineering.**[*]

[*] *Words that appear in **bold** are explained in the glossary on page 60.*

Through genetic engineering we shall soon be able to provide much better treatments, and possibly even cures, for certain serious diseases. We shall be able to create new kinds of life, or altered versions of existing animals and plants, for medical and industrial use, or for improving the environment. But although this powerful new tool promises to do much that is good, it also presents some dangers.

Our bodies are able to fight back against many of the disease-causing organisms found in nature, but we might have no resistance to a completely new germ that has been genetically engineered. There is the risk that such germs might be released before their long-term effects have been properly understood.

Another concern is that some people might want to "design" their own babies. They might want to use genetic engineering to determine details of their child's future appearance. Today, governments around the world are trying to decide on the rules that future genetic engineers will have to follow.

In this book we will look at how the instructions needed to build a new individual are stored inside every animal and plant. We will learn about the complex chemical known as DNA and how it is arranged in working units called **genes**. We will see how scientists have managed to identify the purpose of certain genes and how they are now able to make changes to genes in the laboratory. Finally, we will look at some of the possible benefits and problems that genetic engineering may bring.

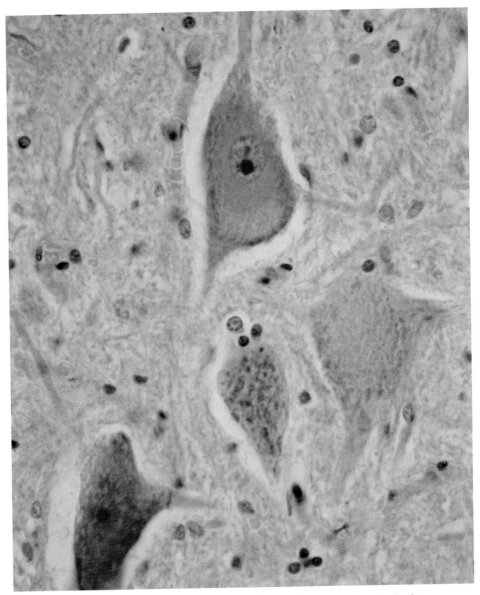

These particular cells, in which the nuclei can be seen as dark dots, have been taken from a person's spinal cord.

CHAPTER 1

The World Inside the Cell

Elephants, oak trees, ants, and human beings may look very different from one another, but like all living things they contain the same fundamental working parts. These working parts are called **cells**.

An adult's body contains about 100 trillion cells that, individually, are too small to be seen without a microscope. Each cell has properties that make it ideally suited to a particular task. A nerve cell, for instance, which carries messages to and from the brain, is long and thin, like a fine wire. A muscle cell, on the other hand, can change shape and is very elastic. At first sight, nerve cells look nothing like muscle cells. However, their basic structure is the same.

All animal and plant cells have three important parts in common. They are surrounded by a clear, flexible covering,

CELL

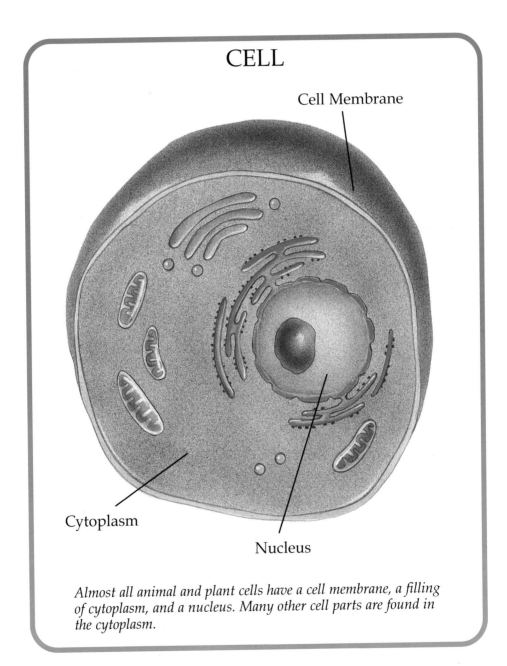

Cell Membrane

Cytoplasm

Nucleus

Almost all animal and plant cells have a cell membrane, a filling of cytoplasm, and a nucleus. Many other cell parts are found in the cytoplasm.

This scientist is adding droplets of a solution containing DNA to a flask.

called a **cell membrane**, inside which is a jelly-like filling, or **cytoplasm**. Within the cytoplasm is the most important part of all—a small, dark speck known as the **nucleus**.

Inside the Nucleus

The nucleus directs the making of essential substances, called **proteins**, on which all life depends. Chemical messages sent out by the nucleus inform the rest of the cell how to put together the required proteins. These proteins then enable the cell to process food into energy, to grow and divide, and to carry out repairs. The instructions needed to make proteins are stored within a special, complex chemical found inside the nucleus, called **DNA**.

DNA is shaped like a twisted rope ladder. The rungs of the ladder are made up of four chemical bases. They are called adenine (A), thymine (T), guanine (G), and cytosine (C), each of which has a different shape, like a piece from a jigsaw puzzle. A and T are shaped so that they fit together exactly. C and G also form a perfectly matched pair. But any other combination, such as A and G, will not lock together. The rungs of the DNA rope ladder, then, are made of A-T and C-G pairs.

In Morse code, letters are represented by series of dots and dashes. Since letters make up words and words make up sentences, Morse code provides a way of representing any amount of information with just two symbols. The A-T and C-G pairs are like chemical dots and dashes. They enable long, coded instructions to be stored in a simple way inside a length of DNA.

The Workings of the Cell

By following the instructions stored in its DNA, a cell is able to manufacture a great variety of chemicals. Thousands of different proteins have to be produced constantly inside your body to help you stay alive and healthy. Proteins make up most of your muscles. They help you digest your food. Even your fingernails and hair are built up from a tough kind of protein called keratin.

DNA

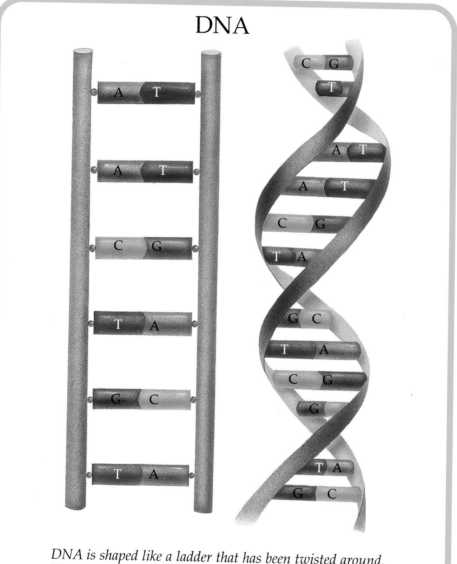

DNA is shaped like a ladder that has been twisted around. The rungs are made of pairs of chemical bases. C always goes with G and A always goes with T.

Like DNA, proteins are highly complex substances. They consist of long chains of smaller chemical units called **amino acids**. Only 20 different amino acids occur in nature. But just as all the words in the English language are made from only 26 letters, many thousands of proteins can result from different combinations of the basic amino acid set.

It is the order of amino acids that gives a protein its special properties, making it, for example, a flower, root, muscle, or skin protein. The instructions stored in the DNA chemical code are used to put the amino acid units into the correct order to make every kind of protein found in cells.

DNA in Action

When a protein needs to be made, a section of the DNA spiral unravels and pulls apart. One side of the unwound DNA acts as the pattern for a particular protein. This protein is assembled, in a long chain, from amino acid "links."

Each amino acid is represented in the DNA code by its own special group of three base units. For example, ACC is the code for one particular amino acid, AAG is the code for another, and so on. Looking along an unwound length of DNA, we could read off its base units in groups of three. By following along, we could read off the sequence of amino acids, and therefore the protein, it specifies. A section of DNA that has the complete code for a single protein is called a gene.

HOW THE DNA CODE HELPS TO MAKE A PROTEIN

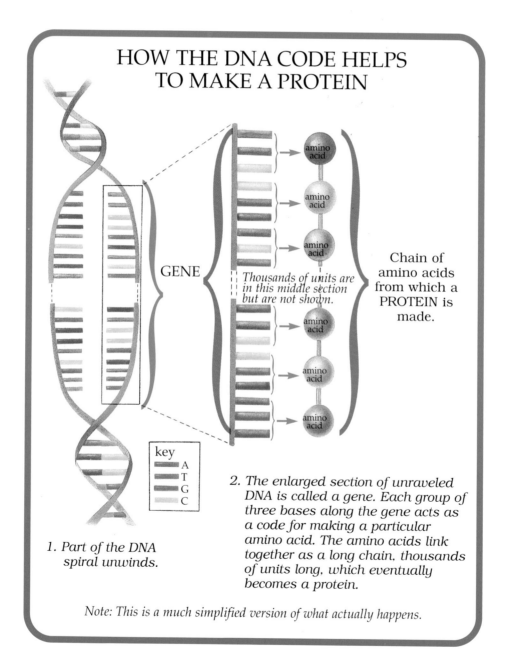

GENE

Thousands of units are in this middle section but are not shown.

amino acid

amino acid

amino acid

amino acid

amino acid

amino acid

Chain of amino acids from which a PROTEIN is made.

key

A
T
G
C

2. The enlarged section of unraveled DNA is called a gene. Each group of three bases along the gene acts as a code for making a particular amino acid. The amino acids link together as a long chain, thousands of units long, which eventually becomes a protein.

1. Part of the DNA spiral unwinds.

Note: This is a much simplified version of what actually happens.

Shown here is a full set of normal female chromosomes arranged in numbered pairs according to a standard classification. The male set differs only in the sex chromosomes (far left), which would include a Y instead of one of the X chromosomes.

Genes determine the type of proteins our bodies make. Genes, therefore, control a huge variety of factors that help make us unique individuals. Genes play a part in determining everything from the color of your hair and eyes to the size of your feet. And since nobody (unless you have an identical twin) has exactly the same set of genes as you have, nobody looks exactly like you, either.

Genes are not found as separate bits of DNA inside the nuclei of our cells. Instead, they are strung out like beads on long strands of DNA known as **chromosomes**. Nearly all of the cells in your body contain 46 chromosomes, arranged in 23 pairs. Each chromosome has thousands of genes strung out along it. If all the DNA making up the chromosomes inside one of your cells were unraveled and joined end to end, the DNA would stretch out almost two yards. All the DNA from all your cells, joined end to end, would reach from the earth to the sun and back about 250 times.

Each cell in your body contains the complete set of DNA needed to make a perfect copy of yourself. If all the information in this DNA were printed out as instructions in English, it would fill a set of encyclopedias with about a million pages. But not every cell in your body uses every instruction on the DNA in its nucleus. It is one of the most remarkable facts of nature

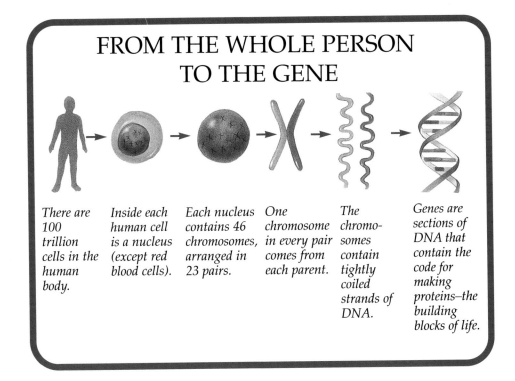

FROM THE WHOLE PERSON TO THE GENE

There are 100 trillion cells in the human body.

Inside each human cell is a nucleus (except red blood cells).

Each nucleus contains 46 chromosomes, arranged in 23 pairs.

One chromosome in every pair comes from each parent.

The chromo-somes contain tightly coiled strands of DNA.

Genes are sections of DNA that contain the code for making proteins–the building blocks of life.

that each cell "reads" only those parts of the DNA code needed to manufacture certain proteins.

Inheriting Genes

Most of our cells contain 46 chromosomes. But there are two types of cells in human beings that have only half this number. These are the egg cells in females and the sperm cells in males. When fertilization takes place, a sperm joins with an egg, and the 23 chromosomes from each combine to make a new set of 46.

Of the 46 chromosomes in your normal body cells, then, 23 have been inherited from your mother and 23 from your father. This means that all the genes on your chromosomes come in two versions, one set inherited from each of your parents.

In the case of some genes, only one of the two versions of the gene is ever used. This is the **dominant** gene. The other member of the pair is said to be **recessive**. In the case of the other genes, the instructions of two corresponding genes may be combined. The overall effect of the two types of genes is that you are, in some ways, like one parent; in other ways, like the other parent; and you have some features that combine traits of both your parents.

Most people have genes that work correctly throughout their lives and cause no serious health problems. But not everyone is so lucky. Genes that are abnormal can give rise to a variety of inherited illnesses, or **genetic diseases**.

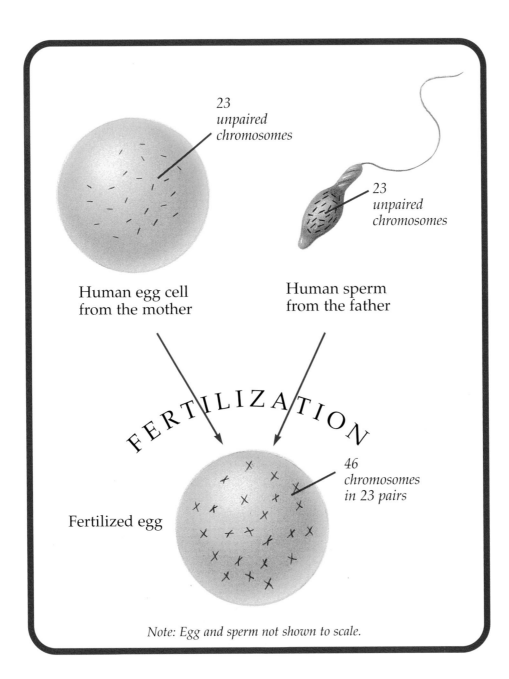

23
unpaired
chromosomes

23
unpaired
chromosomes

Human egg cell
from the mother

Human sperm
from the father

FERTILIZATION

46
chromosomes
in 23 pairs

Fertilized egg

Note: Egg and sperm not shown to scale.

SOLVING THE MYSTERY OF DNA

Working like detectives, scientists gradually uncovered enough clues to be able to solve the mystery of DNA's structure. By the early part of the twentieth century, it was known that DNA has three components: a sugar, an acid, and four different bases (A, T, G, and C). In 1949, the Austro-American biochemist Erwin Chargaff discovered that in any sample of DNA there is always an equal amount of the bases A and T and of the bases G and C. In the early 1950's experiments using X-ray beams, by Rosalind Franklin at the University of London, showed that DNA is a long, thin molecule coiled in a spiral, or helix. Franklin's role in determining the makeup of DNA was far more important than is sometimes recognized. Finally, in 1953, James Watson and Francis Crick of the Cavendish Laboratory in Cambridge, England, put all of the scientific evidence together and worked out DNA's precise structure. From Chargaff's results, Watson and Crick deduced that base A was probably always paired with base T and that base G was always paired with C. This pattern could only happen, they realized, if DNA was composed of two strands twisted together to form a "double helix." The bases form the rungs, and the sugar and the acid make up the sides.

James Watson (left) and Francis Crick (right) next to the first model they made of the structure of DNA in 1953

Inheriting Disease

In the United States alone, 30,000 young people suffer from a serious disease called **cystic fibrosis** (CF). Children with this condition produce a thick, sticky mucus that can clog the air passages of their lungs. The buildup of mucus also makes it easier for harmful bacteria to multiply and cause life-threatening infections.

At present, the treatments available for CF do not make the disease go away. But by simply helping to break up the mucus or by killing some of the germs that breed in it, the treatments reduce the chances of infection. A person suffering from the disease must have regular physiotherapy. This involves being rubbed on the chest and clapped on the back so that the mucus is loosened and can be coughed up. A variety of medications can also be given to help control the amount of

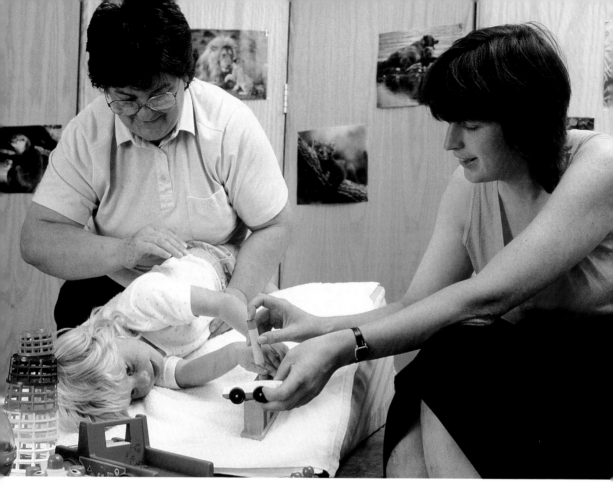

A three-year-old child with cystic fibrosis receives treatment from a physiotherapist. Rubbing and clapping on the back and chest loosens the mucus, which is coughed up,

mucus and limit the spread of bacteria. Even so, few people affected with this condition live much beyond age 30.

Cystic fibrosis is a genetic disease. It is passed on to a child through the genes of its parents. Until recently, no one knew which gene or genes among the many thousands contained in a person's DNA were responsible for the disease. But in June 1989 a team of Canadian and American scientists found the single gene that is responsible for CF. Now, it is hoped, this

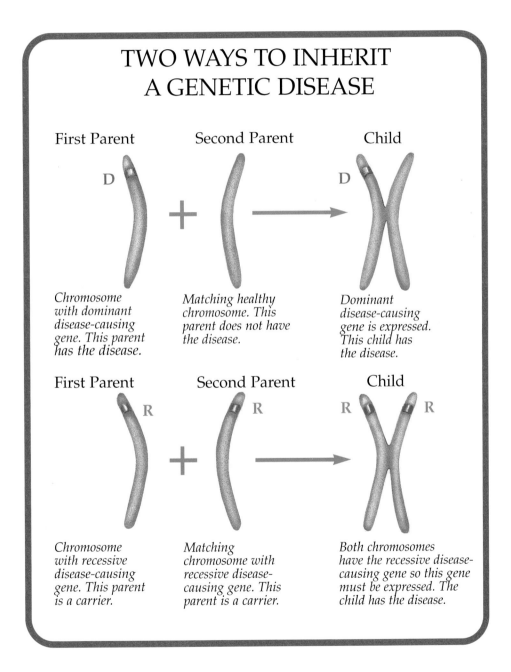

TWO WAYS TO INHERIT A GENETIC DISEASE

First Parent

D

Chromosome with dominant disease-causing gene. This parent has the disease.

Second Parent

Matching healthy chromosome. This parent does not have the disease.

Child

D

Dominant disease-causing gene is expressed. This child has the disease.

First Parent

R

Chromosome with recessive disease-causing gene. This parent is a carrier.

Second Parent

R

Matching chromosome with recessive disease-causing gene. This parent is a carrier.

Child

R   R

Both chromosomes have the recessive disease-causing gene so this gene must be expressed. The child has the disease.

breakthrough will lead to the possibility of earlier **diagnosis** and more effective forms of treatment.

Genes from Our Parents

To understand how genetic diseases come about, remember that all genes (except those in egg and sperm cells) occur in pairs. One member of each pair comes from the mother and one from the father.

Nearly all individuals have a few disease-causing genes among their DNA. For example, among Caucasians (white-skinned people), about 1 person in 20 is thought to carry the gene responsible for cystic fibrosis. But normally this does not matter. Because the disease-causing gene is almost always recessive, its instructions are rarely used. Instead, its dominant twin, which in most cases is healthy, is the one that is "switched on."

Inherited diseases are of two types. The first are those resulting from a disease-causing dominant gene inherited from either the father or the mother. In this case, the parent who passes on the unhealthy gene must also be a sufferer of the disease.

The second type of genetic disease comes about when a child receives the same disease-causing recessive gene from both parents. Since there is now no choice but for one of the unhealthy genes to be switched on, the child will suffer from the disease. Cystic fibrosis is caused in this way.

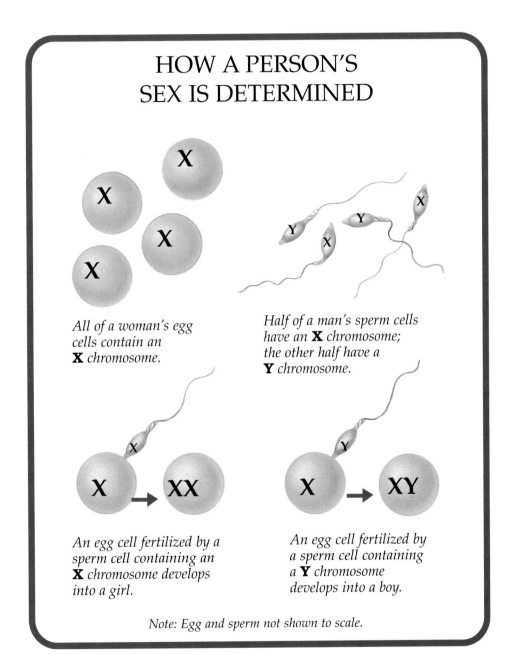

HOW A PERSON'S SEX IS DETERMINED

All of a woman's egg cells contain an **X** *chromosome.*

Half of a man's sperm cells have an **X** *chromosome; the other half have a* **Y** *chromosome.*

An egg cell fertilized by a sperm cell containing an **X** *chromosome develops into a girl.*

An egg cell fertilized by a sperm cell containing a **Y** *chromosome develops into a boy.*

Note: Egg and sperm not shown to scale.

Troubles with X

Just one special chromosome makes the difference between whether you are a boy or a girl. If you are a girl, the chromosomes from each of your body cells could be sorted into 23 matching pairs. But if you are a boy, your body cells contain only 22 matching pairs. In the other pair, the chromosomes don't look alike—one is shaped like an X, the other is smaller and shaped like a Y.

All of a woman's egg cells contain a single X chromosome. However, half a man's sperm cells have an unpaired X and the other half an unpaired Y. Your sex was determined by whether the egg from which you grew was fertilized by a sperm containing an X chromosome or by a sperm containing a Y chromosome.

Some genetic diseases, said to be **sex-linked**, are caused by unhealthy genes on the X chromosome (never, so far as we know, on the Y). One of these sex-linked diseases is **hemophilia**. A sufferer from this disease has blood that does not clot properly. As a result, even small cuts and bruises, if left untreated, can lead to serious bleeding.

Because hemophilia is caused by a recessive gene on the X chromosome, a woman who has the hemophilia gene on just one of her X chromosomes in her normal body cells will not show any signs of the disorder. She will, however, be a **carrier**. This means that she can pass on the disease-causing gene to her offspring. Any male child who inherits the hemophilia gene on his mother's X chromosome will have the disease. As a result, there is a high risk (1 in 2) of a boy having hemophilia if his mother is a carrier. A girl's chance of inheriting the disease is very low. For a girl to be a sufferer, both the X chromosome she received from her mother and the X chromosome she received from her father would have to contain the gene responsible for hemophilia.

People who have a family history of inherited disease can be given advice on how likely they are to pass on a genetic disorder to their children. This advice is called **genetic counseling**.

To see if a person actually has any disease-causing genes, doctors can carry out a variety of tests. Such tests are known collectively as **genetic screening**.

Testing Before Birth

A developed but unborn child, or **fetus**, can undergo prenatal (before-birth) screening to give some idea of the chance that it will inherit a genetic disease from its parents. Such screening cannot, however, give information on whether a disease will show itself early or late in life, or whether the child will be mildly or severely disabled.

One of the tests carried out before birth, known as **amniocentesis**, is done 14 to 15 weeks after the mother becomes pregnant. An ultrasound scanner, which gives off very high-pitched sound waves, is used to form a moving TV picture of the fluid-filled bag (the amnion) that surrounds the fetus. The doctor then draws off a small sample of the fluid with a hypodermic

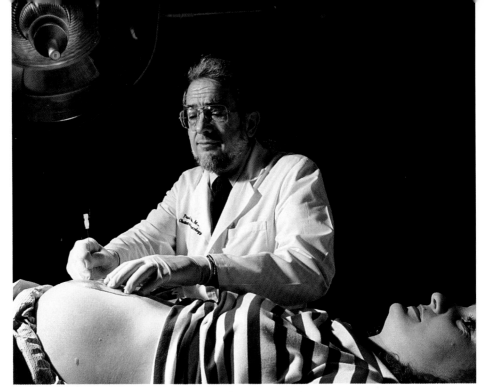

An amniocentesis test being carried out in early pregnancy

needle. Inside the sample will be a few cells from the fetus. DNA from these cells can be examined to see if it contains any disease-causing genes.

A more recently developed method of obtaining cells from a fetus is called **CVS** (chorion villus sampling). This test allows doctors to detect serious genetic diseases in a fetus that is only 8 to 10 weeks old. Guided by an ultrasound scanner, doctors take some of the cells from the place (the chorion) where the young fetus is joined to the mother's body. The extracted substance gives enough DNA from the fetus for results to be obtained in a day or two. In contrast, the older technique of amniocentesis provides only a few cells, which are allowed to reproduce themselves in the laboratory until they form a big enough sample. This process can delay the outcome of the test by several weeks.

One of the advantages of prenatal genetic screening is that it offers a family a chance to prepare for the special needs of a child who may have a genetic disease. Such preparation might include talking to other parents of children with the same disorder and joining a support group.

A Matter of Life and Death

Prenatal screening also raises a very controversial issue. On learning that her unborn baby may develop a genetic disease, an expectant mother might decide to have an **abortion**. There is great disagreement in the United States and in other countries about whether abortions should be carried out under any circumstances. And there is a particular debate about whether abortions should be performed to prevent the births of children with physical or mental disabilities caused by genetic disease.

Eventually, this problem is likely to be made more complicated because of a technique called in vitro fertilization (IVF). IVF allows egg cells from a woman and sperm cells from a man to be brought together in the laboratory. Usually a number of fertilized cells develop in the laboratory, and one is chosen by the doctor to be placed inside the mother to develop into a baby. (The technique has given rise to the expression "test-tube babies.")

In the future, it will be possible to screen each of the fertilized eggs for disease-causing genes. When a fertilized egg without any disease-causing genes is found, the doctor will be able to implant this in the mother. It remains for society to

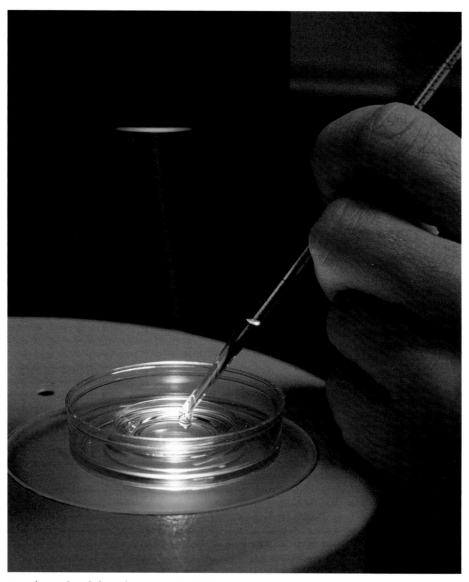

In vitro fertilization. *At the IVF unit in a London hospital, a technician looks through a microscope at egg cells and sperm in a dish to check for successful fertilization.*

decide whether such selection should be legal and how far choosing the genetic characteristics of children, in general, should be allowed.

TRACKING DOWN THE CAUSES OF GENETIC DISEASE

How do researchers pinpoint which gene is responsible for a particular disease? The task may seem like looking for a needle in a haystack, when you consider that our 46 chromosomes contain around 100,000 genes, any one of which might be the culprit. In the case of some disorders, the search is made easier because the chromosomes on which a particular gene lies may be partly absent in sufferers of the disease. Such missing bits of DNA help to narrow down the area of the chromosome that must carry the crucial gene in healthy individuals. In the case of other genetic disorders,

all the chromosomes appear complete. Researchers then have to study samples of DNA taken from many individuals—parents, children, grandparents, cousins—from families in which a particular disease tends to occur. This technique allows sections of DNA called "markers" to be identified. Markers lie on either side of the disease-causing gene. The closer a marker is to the required gene, the more likely it is that both the marker and the gene will be passed down from generation to generation. Through careful analysis, over a number of years, scientists have used this method to track down the specific genes responsible for diseases such as cystic fibrosis.

This researcher is working under an ultraviolet light while preparing a gel used in the separation of DNA. The visor is worn to shield the eyes from the UV light.

CHAPTER 3

Gene Therapy: Hopes and Fears

One infant in every hundred is born with a serious genetic disease or condition. Usually the problem becomes obvious to parents and doctors quite early in a child's life. All too often, the disease results in physical or mental disabilities, prolonged and severe pain, and a shortened life. More than 4,000 inherited disorders are known. But until now, most have lacked fully effective treatments.

It is no wonder, then, that scientists have long imagined being able to treat or even cure inherited diseases by replacing the disease-causing genes in a patient's body with healthy ones. Today, these exciting developments are just beginning to take place. In the future, they will become increasingly important.

Scientists are tracking down more and more of the genes responsible for the various inherited diseases that afflict

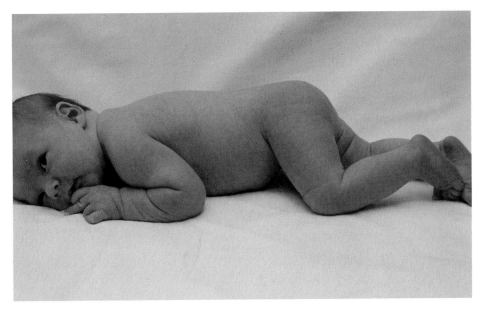

A healthy 6-day-old baby

human beings. A new and important field of medicine, known as **gene therapy**, is opening up.

Targets for Therapy

Among the commonest of genetic disorders is Down syndrome. Children born with Down syndrome are mentally disabled. The cause of the condition is that their body cells contain 47 chromosomes instead of the usual 46.

Most inherited conditions, however, do not result from problems with whole chromosomes but with tiny parts of them. In fact, a number of common genetic diseases are caused by just one unhealthy gene. It is these single-gene disorders, such as *cystic fibrosis* and *hemophilia*, that promise to be the simplest to treat by gene therapy.

Another condition caused by a single disease-causing gene is known as *severe combined immunodeficiency*, or **SCID**. Children with SCID do not have enough white blood cells. These cells are produced in the **bone marrow** and are one of the body's main lines of defense. White blood cells recognize and destroy foreign particles, such as bacteria, that invade the bloodstream. People who don't have an adequate supply of white blood cells cannot fight infections.

In about a quarter of all SCID cases, the problem lies with a gene that carries the code for making a protein called ADA. If this gene is faulty or missing, all of the cells in a person's body are slightly damaged because they cannot manufacture the ADA they need. The most seriously affected cells, however, are in the bone marrow. Without ADA, a person's bone marrow cells cannot make healthy white blood cells.

The ADA gene was among the first to be linked to a particular genetic disorder. In 1990, at the National Institutes of Health in Bethesda, Maryland, the ADA gene became the target of the world's first trial of gene therapy on a human being. The patient was a four-year-old girl.

New Genes for Old

One way that doctors can carry out gene therapy is by using viruses. Normally, viruses cause disease. They do this by attacking cells in the body and inserting their own genes into the DNA of the cells. The infected body cell now has instructions to make more copies of the virus. Eventually, these copies burst out, killing the infected cell. Then they go on to attack other cells.

Specially altered viruses, however, can be valuable because they provide a means of delivering healthy genes into a patient's body cells. The first step in preparing a virus for use in gene therapy is to make it safe. This involves changing the virus so that it cannot be reproduced and so destroy the cells it enters. The second step is to add to the virus a healthy gene. This is the method currently being used in the gene therapy for SCID.

Doctors add a healthy ADA gene, taken from a normal human cell, to a special kind of virus called a **retrovirus**. Retroviruses are used in gene therapy because they have a very simple genetic structure and are, therefore, easy to work with. The altered retrovirus is added to a sample of **stem cells** taken from the bone marrow of a child suffering from SCID. Stem cells are the cells from which white blood cells develop.

Each retrovirus fixes itself to a stem cell and releases its genes into the cell. The healthy ADA gene from the retrovirus becomes "stitched" in to the DNA inside the cell's nucleus so that the stem cell can now make normal amounts of ADA.

When large numbers of stem cells in the sample taken from the patient have been changed by the virus, they are injected back into the patient's bone marrow. Because they now produce their own ADA, the stem cells can develop into

VIRUSES

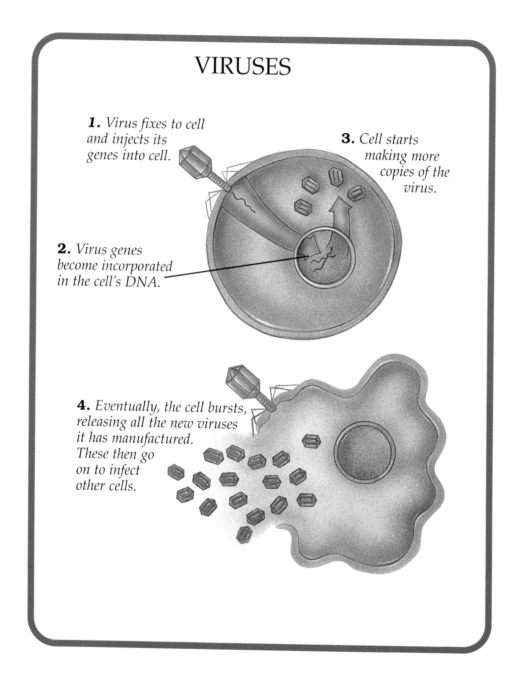

1. Virus fixes to cell and injects its genes into cell.

3. Cell starts making more copies of the virus.

2. Virus genes become incorporated in the cell's DNA.

4. Eventually, the cell bursts, releasing all the new viruses it has manufactured. These then go on to infect other cells.

white blood cells as they would in a healthy person. One treatment results in enough white blood cells to help the patient fight off infections for two to three months. Then the process has to be repeated. Today, several children with SCID in the United States and Great Britain are benefiting from this form of treatment.

Future Progress in Gene Therapy

Taking living cells from a patient, replacing disease-causing genes, and then putting the altered cells back into the patient's body is called **augmentation therapy**. This is likely to be the commonest form of gene therapy in use for a number of years to come. However, it cannot provide a permanent cure for genetic disease because too many of the patient's cells remain untreated.

Lasting cures for genetic disease will involve more advanced forms of gene therapy. Ideally, doctors would like to be able to take out the faulty genes from every cell in all or part of a patient's body and put healthy genes in their place. No one yet knows how to do this successfully. In the future, researchers may find a way to deliver replacement genes to many millions of different cells inside the human body. Special chemicals or viruses, for example, could be used to deliver the genes to the right places in the body.

Simply getting a healthy gene into a cell, however, is not the end of the problem. A gene will work only if its coded instructions are read by the cell. This can happen only if the bits of DNA on either side of the gene, which are like punctuation marks (called "codons"), are properly positioned and undamaged. Another problem is that a new gene that finds its way into the wrong part of a chromosome could act as a trigger for cancer. In time, these complications may be overcome. Meanwhile, doctors and lawmakers are trying to come to grips with some of the difficult ethical questions raised by gene therapy.

Rules to Live By

Gene therapy is so new that no one can really be sure what long-term effects it might have. Experiments conducted on animals have shown that changes to faulty genes can sometimes be carried out safely and successfully. However, when an error is made, it can lead to a further genetic disease in the animal and its offspring. Because of this, some specialists argue that gene therapy has not been tested fully enough for these experiments to be continued on human beings.

So far, gene therapy trials on children with SCID have involved making changes to ordinary body cells, not to reproductive cells. The altered ADA gene is not able to leave the white blood cells and find its way into the DNA in egg and sperm cells. This distinction is very important. Many doctors think it is acceptable to replace a disease-causing gene in a single individual. But because the long-term effects of gene therapy are still unknown, opinion is divided about making genetic changes that would be passed on to future generations.

Setbacks and Surprises

Recently, it has become clear that even single-gene diseases may prove much harder to treat than was originally expected. The gene that causes cystic fibrosis, for instance, has been found to come in hundreds of slightly different forms, called **mutations**.

With so many possible mutations, the number of combinations in a person who inherits one CF gene from each parent is almost endless. Researchers are finding that pairings of different mutations produce different effects. Some pairings may cause severe cystic fibrosis, while others lead to less serious disorders like asthma or bronchitis. It also seems that other genes could affect the way different mutations of the CF gene behave. For instance, a pair of mutations inherited by one person might behave differently from the same pair inherited by another person, depending on the state of a third, controlling gene.

These discoveries make the task of genetic counseling much more difficult. Counseling can still be expected to make reliable predictions in the case of a family that has a known history of CF. But doctors now believe it may be much riskier to offer opinions about individuals who have no family history of the disease or who have inherited a pair of mutations that scientists are still unfamiliar with.

CHAPTER 4

⚬ Designer Genes

One of the greatest scientific ventures under way at present is called the Human Genome Project. Its goal is to map the position of every one of the 100,000 or so genes strung out along the 23 pairs of human chromosomes. This endeavor is expected to last until about the year 2005, to cost several billion dollars, and to involve hundreds of scientists from countries around the world.

If the Human Genome Project is successful, it will mark a great leap forward in our knowledge of the causes of genetic disease. By early in the twenty-first century, scientists may be able to pinpoint exactly which genes are responsible for many of the genetic disorders that afflict human beings. This information will be used by gene therapists to improve greatly the understanding of diseases such as cystic fibrosis, hemophilia,

This scientist is working in a large laboratory in France dedicated to mapping the human genome.

sickle-cell anemia (another blood disorder), and **muscular dystrophy** (a condition in which a person's muscles gradually waste away). Improved knowledge of the location of particular genes will help scientists develop better treatments and eventually, perhaps, find permanent cures for these diseases.

Along with the benefits that gene therapy may bring, however, there are dangers. In time, scientists may be able to make widespread changes to a person's DNA. Genetic engineering may even progress to the point where it becomes possible to design how a future human being will look.

Dream Babies

Gene therapy and genetic engineering raise some important concerns. Few people would doubt the value of gene therapy that can cure a serious disease such as cystic fibrosis. But there is uncertainty over how much tampering should be allowed with an individual's genetic makeup. Should gene therapy, for instance, be used to correct minor genetic ailments like color blindness? Should it be used to ensure that people do not grow up with crooked teeth or flat feet?

If minor genetic conditions are eventually treated by gene therapy, people may be tempted to go a step further. Some parents may wish to use genetic engineering to select their baby's appearance.

Height, the color of eyes, hair, and skin, shoe size, muscle build, and many other physical characteristics are determined, in part, by the coded instructions in our genes. But should it be lawful to influence how a future human being will look by altering a child's genes before birth?

Like many developments in science, genetic engineering could be used in ways that are both good and bad for human beings. During the Second World War, Adolf Hitler and other members of Germany's ruling Nazi party sought to extermi-nate whole groups of people—such as Jews, homosexuals, Gypsies, disabled people—whom they considered to have infe-rior genes. The Nazis' goal was to breed a new race of strong, white-skinned, fair-haired people who would rule over every-one else. If, in the future, other evil dictators like Hitler were to rise to power, they might try to use genetic engineering for their own ends.

Mighty Mouse and Beyond

Not surprisingly, many doctors would like to see govern-ments around the world introduce strict rules to control the use of genetic engineering. These rules would prevent altered genes from being passed on to future generations—at least until the altered genes were proved to be safe. The regulations would also ensure that gene therapy was used only to cure dis-eases and not to help determine a person's appearance and other physical characteristics.

The laws governing genetic engineering on human beings are likely to be strict. However, scientists have already carried

The corn plants in this greenhouse have been genetically engineered to resist attack by a pest called the European corn borer.

out wide-ranging genetic experiments on animals and plants. They have created **transgenic animals** and plants by taking genes from one organism and placing them in the DNA of a different kind of creature.

In 1981, researchers took the gene for producing growth hormone in rats and injected it into the fertilized eggs of mice. Growth hormone is a chemical that controls how fast and how much an individual grows. The growth hormone gene from the rats made the injected mice grow to be half as big again as a normal mouse. However, the results of this type of experiment are hard to predict. For example, when the human growth hormone gene was put into the fertilized eggs of pigs, the pigs did not grow larger. Instead, they produced leaner meat and were cross-eyed.

There is much debate about whether experiments should be carried out on animals, particularly if the tests may cause any sort of suffering. Supporters of genetic experiments on animals, however, argue that it is only through research on other species that scientists can develop new forms of gene therapy for human beings.

Living Factories

Animals have been genetically engineered to produce important, rare drugs in their milk. These valuable medicines include insulin, which is needed by people who suffer from diabetes, and antitrypsin, a chemical that can help in the treatment of lung diseases.

This transgenic ewe has been given the human gene that causes the production of a protein called antitrypsin in the sheep's milk. Her lamb is also transgenic for this protein.

To turn an animal into a kind of living drug factory, scientists extract, from a human cell, the gene for making the required substance. Then this gene is placed inside the nucleus of a fertilized egg of an animal, such as a sheep. As the young sheep develops, each of its cells will include a copy of the human gene. Finally, when the sheep has young of its own and produces milk, its milk will contain small amounts of the substance for which the human gene carries the code.

Research is now being done to improve the quantity of various types of drugs produced in animals' milk. The yield of these drugs is expected to increase gradually. By the beginning of the twenty-first century, large stocks of animals such as sheep and cows may have been genetically engineered to produce everything from blood-clotting substances for hemophilia sufferers to human growth hormone.

New Creatures

Through genetic engineering, entirely new kinds of life-forms are being created. These include plants that make their own pesticides, bacteria that boost the fertility of the soil in which they live, and other kinds of bacteria that clean up pollution in oceans and rivers. By placing new genes into existing life-forms, scientists can in effect design creatures to suit specific human needs.

Much good may come from setting genetically engineered organisms free into the environment. Already new kinds of cereal crops, fruits, and vegetables that can resist disease and pests have been developed. Some plants are being designed that can produce their own insecticide. This will allow farmers to use less chemical spray. Eventually crops may be tailored to live in places where there is poor soil or very little rain.

But there are risks. Transgenic animals and plants are unknown in the natural world. No one can be sure what effect these genetically altered life-forms might have on other species. One danger is that a genetically engineered organism might be safe in itself but its altered genes might be transferred to other living things, which may be harmed. Another possibility is that by making plants resistant to some kinds of germs, we will encourage the evolution of other kinds of disease-causing germs.

In the United States, between 1974 and 1976, public concern was so great that all research in genetic engineering was

Researchers have genetically improved tomatoes to reduce the production of a gas called ethylene that causes tomatoes to ripen. When the gene is inserted into the tomato plant, it slows the ripening process. This allows the fruit to reach maturity on the plant, providing consumers with vine-ripened tomatoes year-round.

stopped. Then a set of guidelines was introduced to control possible dangers. Most countries now have similar rules. The first release of genetically engineered organisms, in the form of pesticides, took place in the United States in 1985. Further releases have since taken place under controlled conditions to ensure that the introduction of transgenic animals and plants into the wild is done with the minimum of risk.

In 1994, the first genetically engineered produce went on sale in stores around the United States. This included tomatoes in which the genes had been altered so that the fruit would ripen without rotting. Meanwhile, environmentalists are urging extreme caution before such "unnatural" living things are let out of the laboratory.

HOW TO SOW CRESS AND REAP PLASTIC

In the future, farmers may grow plastics as a crop. Genetic engineers in the United States have altered the genes in a plant known as thale cress so that it produces a natural and totally biodegradable plastic material called PHB.

The researchers took two genes from a kind of bacterium that makes PHB naturally and stores it in the same way that humans store fat. Then they introduced these genes into the cells of a thale cress plant so that it could make its own PHB. One problem is that the altered cress tends to become sickly, perhaps because it uses up so much energy in the production of the plastic. A way around this may be to put the genes into other kinds of plants, such as sugar beets or potatoes, that make great quantities of energy-storing substances like sugar and starch. If further research is successful, the twenty-first century could see farmers reaping harvests of plastic and other substances alongside their fields of corn and cabbage.

CHAPTER 5

Genetic Information: Ownership and Privacy

Who owns your genes? The answer may seem obvious: you do. But the question of who owns what in the world of genetic engineering is not at all clear-cut.

Companies and laboratories involved in developing new kinds of animals and plants by genetic engineering claim that they should be able to patent these new life-forms. A patent gives a person or organization control over a design and the right to decide who else may use that design.

The first transgenic mammal to be registered by the U.S. Patent Office is a mouse that contains a human cancer-causing gene, known as an oncogene. Genetically identical copies of the "onco-mouse" are now offered for sale by a big chemical manufacturing company to researchers studying ways in which certain kinds of cancer start in human beings.

The idea of patenting animals and plants is opposed by some people. It is wrong, these critics believe, to treat living things as if they were inventions. On the other hand, supporters of patenting say that it encourages further valuable work in genetic engineering and gene therapy. Patent holders, their supporters point out, can charge other people for using their inventions. The money the patent holders make provides them with funds for additional research and development.

A Revolution in Knowledge

More and more, specific genes are being identified as the cause of genetic diseases. Just as important, scientists have also found that the occurrence of certain other conditions, such as some kinds of cancer and heart disease, may be influenced in part by the type of genes with which a person is born. For example, women who have a particular gene on what is known as chromosome 17 have a much greater chance of developing breast cancer while young than women who do not carry this gene. It is important to remember, though, that cancer-causing substances in the environment, poor diet, smoking, and lack of exercise are usually more significant than faulty genes as the underlying causes of cancer and heart disease.

Genes that make it more likely that a person will eventually suffer from colon cancer, liver cancer, **arthritis, Alzheimer's disease**, and a number of other quite common illnesses have all recently been found. Alzheimer's disease is a

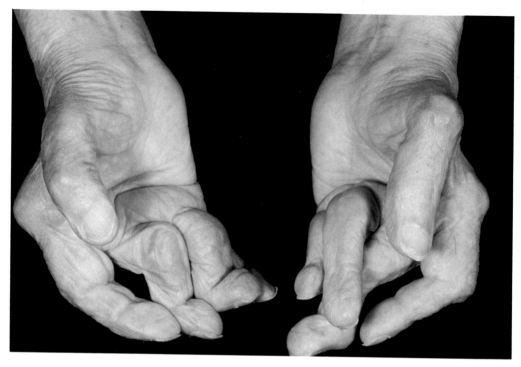

Person suffering from severe arthritis

particularly unpleasant condition. It affects large numbers of people, especially the elderly, and results in a progressive loss of mental and physical powers.

As more becomes known about the genes responsible for various diseases, so the effectiveness of genetic screening as a tool in diagnosis will grow. This is especially true of diseases, such as cystic fibrosis, that are caused by single genes. Screening can be carried out on someone of any age. It can help individuals to know, for instance, whether they carry any faulty genes that could be passed on to their children.

But the increasing effectiveness of genetic screening also raises some difficult issues. As time goes on, employers will look more and more to genetic screening as a way of checking

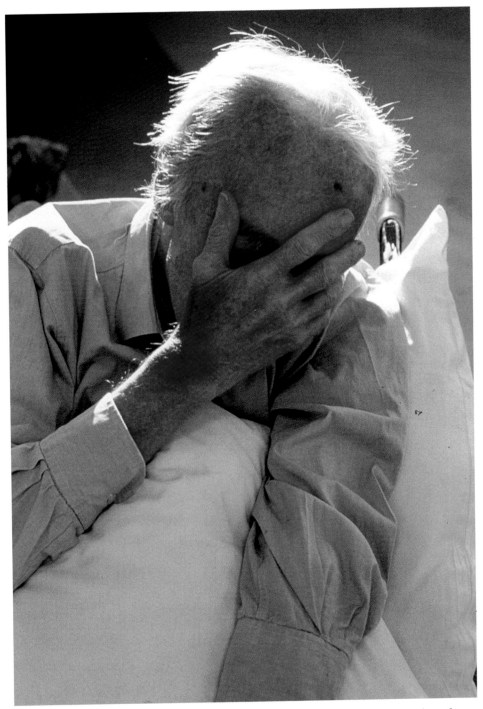

An elderly man with Alzheimer's disease hides his face with his hand.

whether future employees will suffer from any genetically linked diseases that could affect their work. This use of genetic screening is seen as a serious threat to people's privacy.

Genes and Privacy

Genetic screening can only be used to predict whether a person *might* develop a genetic disease. It gives probabilities, not certainties. However, as genetic screening becomes increasingly common, there is the danger that many people will find themselves the victims of discrimination. Suppose, for example, that a screening test shows that a person has the single faulty gene responsible for **Huntington's chorea**. This disease shows itself first in middle age; the effects usually become noticeable at about age 35 or 40. Thereafter, it leads to a steady breakdown in the sufferer's physical and mental health.

A potential employer who found out that a job applicant carried the gene which causes Huntington's chorea might be reluctant to hire that person. In fact, such situations have already happened. A graduate of a police academy in the Midwest was about to be hired as a police officer when it became known that he had a family history of Huntington's chorea. The man was told he would have to be tested for the gene responsible for the disease before he could be accepted.

Similar incidents are likely to be more common in the future as genetic screening becomes widespread. New laws will need to be enacted to protect individuals' rights.

Genetic Disease and Insurance

Health insurance companies also have a great interest in people's genes. Someone suffering from a serious genetic disorder is likely to make large health insurance claims. Because of this, company officials argue that they should have access to genetic information on the people they insure or might insure. But such knowledge could make the insurers refuse to provide coverage to people they think are at high risk for genetic disease.

Already people either have been denied insurance coverage or have received less in insurance payments because they or their dependents have genetic disorders. As genetic screening becomes a more efficient predictor of disease, such discrimination is likely to increase. At present, individuals are not protected by any federal law from insurance companies that discriminate against them because of their genes. Some states, however, including Arizona, Florida, and Wisconsin, have passed laws to protect people against such discrimination. Other states, like California, New York, Ohio, and Wyoming, are set to follow suit.

There is another, equally disturbing danger. The high cost of insuring children who prenatal screening suggests might develop genetic diseases could lead to more abortions. One insurance company has already put pressure on parents to abort fetuses with disabilities by threatening to cancel their insurance policies. Some doctors and politicians believe that laws must be introduced to ensure that people have the right to keep information about their genes, and the genes of their offspring, strictly private if they wish to do so.

The Future

It is clear that the new techniques of genetic engineering and gene therapy will solve some important problems while at the same time creating others. Yet, overall, the human race stands to gain much from its increasing knowledge of how to alter the DNA code.

Within 50 years, many of today's most devastating illnesses may be not only treatable but curable. Cystic fibrosis, hemophilia, and other such ailments may disappear entirely. Other diseases that are in part related to faulty genes, such as some types of cancer, heart disease, and Alzheimer's disease, may become more easily treatable.

Thanks to genetic engineering, countless new kinds of plants and animals will serve the human race in all sorts of ways. Some varieties of plants will produce plastics and other substances for industrial purposes. Other new strains of plants may be placed on the sides of busy roads to absorb poisonous gases given off by cars and trucks. Plants with altered genes might even help reduce the greenhouse effect by absorbing more carbon dioxide from the air. Meanwhile, transgenic animals will produce valuable medicines in their milk or thrive in places that are highly polluted.

How much human beings will be genetically engineered in the years to come is not at all clear. What is certain is that the choices and laws we as a society make now will have an immense effect on all our futures.

BRINGING BACK THE DINOSAURS?

In the film *Jurassic Park*, scientists bring dinosaurs back to life and then place them in the ultimate theme park. The story of how they are able to do this is cleverly thought out. First, over 100 million years ago, an insect bites and sucks some blood from a living dinosaur. The insect lands on a tree and gets caught in a sticky trickle of resin. Over a long period of time, the resin hardens and turns into a piece of yellow amber. Eventually scientists find the amber with the insect perfectly pre-served inside. They extract the dinosaur DNA from the blood in the insect's body and use its coded instructions to bring the dinosaur back to life. Entertaining though this idea may be, it will probably always remain in the realm of fantasy. Tiny fragments of insect DNA have, in fact, been extracted from fossils embedded in amber. But the amber does not preserve the creature's soft parts or any of its body fluids. Because of this, any dinosaur DNA that may once have been inside the insect has long ago broken down and been lost.

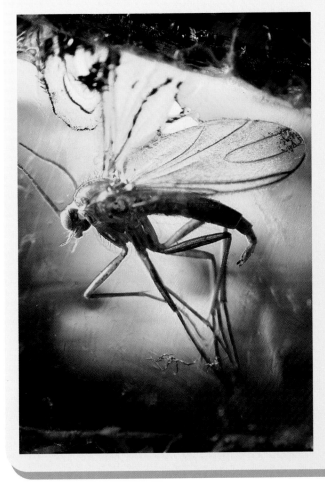

This fossilized fly, a relative of today's mosquito, is embedded in amber that is about 40 million years old.

Glossary

abortion — (1) the intentional ending of a pregnancy, or (2) the natural ejection of a young fetus or embryo from a mother's body

Alzheimer's disease — a disease in which large numbers of brain cells are destroyed, resulting in a progressive loss of memory and other mental capabilities. The disorder is believed to have a genetic basis.

amino acids — simple chemical units found in all living things. They combine to make up proteins.

amniocentesis — a technique for analyzing the genes of a fetus. The test involves sampling the fluid in which the fetus is located.

arthritis — a disease that causes painful swelling of one or more joints

augmentation therapy — a form of gene therapy in which cells with healthy genes are introduced into a patient's body to help supply a missing protein

bone marrow — the soft substance that fills the middle of long bones and in which blood cells are made

carrier — a person with a disease-causing recessive gene who does not have the disease but who can pass it on to his or her children. If both parents contribute recessive genes, the child is likely to have the disease.

cell — the basic unit that makes up all living things and carries out all of an organism's functions

cell membrane — the flexible outer covering that surrounds an animal or plant cell and controls the passage of chemicals into or out of the cell

chromosomes — the thread-like structures in the nucleus of cells. They carry information about the nature and function of the cell.

CVS—short for chorion villus sampling, a technique for analyzing the genes of a very young fetus. It involves taking a sample of cells from the chorion—the structure that joins the fetus to the mother.

cystic fibrosis—an inherited condition in which the sufferer produces large amounts of thick, sticky mucus. The mucus acts as a breeding ground for potentially dangerous bacteria and must be cleared regularly.

cytoplasm—the jelly-like material surrounding the nucleus of a cell. It contains the structures that produce the chemicals needed by the cell.

diagnosis—the identification of a disease or the cause of an ailment

DNA—short for deoxyribonucleic acid. One of the two nucleic acids found in the nuclei of cells. This molecule decides the composition of proteins.

dominant—describes something that controls or is stronger than something else

fetus—an unborn child from the end of the eighth week of pregnancy to the moment of birth. Before the eighth week the unborn child is known as an embryo.

gene—the sequence of DNA that contains the code for a specific protein

gene therapy—the process of altering the genetic code in diseased cells to repair genetic defects

genetic counseling—advice given to potential parents about the chances that their offspring will inherit certain genetic disorders

genetic disease—a disorder caused by missing or faulty genes

genetic engineering—the science of altering genetic codes in the cells of living things to produce a change in appearance or function

genetic screening—the process of examining the genes of an individual, before or after birth, to predict any genetic diseases

hemophilia—an inherited condition in which the sufferer's blood lacks a substance that causes clotting

Glossary

Huntington's chorea—a genetic disease that causes a progressive break-down of physical and mental health. Its effects usually start in victims around age 35 or 40.

muscular dystrophy—a genetic disease that results in a gradual weakening of a person's muscles

mutation—an accidental change in the DNA making up a gene or chromosome. Mutations can be caused, for example, by exposure to penetrating radiation or certain chemicals. Only if the sperm or egg cells are affected can these changes be passed on to the next generation.

nucleus—the place where DNA is stored inside an animal or plant cell. Instructions that control the production of proteins are issued from the nucleus.

proteins—a group of substances that are the basis of every cell. Proteins, which are very complex, are made up of hundreds or thousands of combinations of amino acids.

recessive—describes something that is pushed back by, or weaker than, something else

retrovirus—a simple kind of virus that contains only about ten genes

SCID—short for severe combined immunodeficiency, a genetic disease in which few or no white blood cells are manufactured to protect the body against infection

sex-linked—having to do with the sex chromosomes, X and Y

sickle-cell anemia—a blood disease caused by a faulty gene that prevents blood cells from forming correctly. The abnormal cells are unable to carry oxygen properly.

stem cell—a young cell that has not yet developed into a special-purpose cell

transgenic animal (or plant)—a new type of organism created by mixing together the genes from existing animals or plants

For Further Reading

Asimov, Isaac. *How Did We Find Out About DNA?* (How Did We Find Out About . . . series). Walker & Co., 1985.

Bains, William. *Genetic Engineering for Almost Everyone*. Viking Penguin, 1988.

Balkwill, Frances, and Rolph, Mic. *Amazing Schemes Within Your Genes*. HarperCollins, 1993.

Balkwill, Frances, and Rolph, Mic. *DNA Is Here to Stay*. HarperCollins, 1992.

Bender, Lionel. *Atoms and Cells*. Watts, 1989.

Bornstein, Sandy. *What Makes You What You Are: A First Look at Genetics*. J. Messner, 1989.

Bycynski, Lynn. *Genetics: Nature's Blueprint* (Encyclopedia of Discovery and Invention series). Lucent Books, 1991.

Gutnik, Martin. *Genetics Projects for Young Scientists*. Watts, 1989.

Higgins, Jane H. *Discovering Genetics* (The Discovery series). DOK Publications, 1983.

Lampton, Christopher. *Gene Technology: Confronting the Issues* (Science, Technology and Society series). Watts, 1990.

Sayre, Anne. *Rosalind Franklin and DNA*. Norton, 1978.

Wilcox, Frank H. *DNA: The Thread of Life* (Discovery! series). Lerner Publications, 1988.

Index